ZAN MITREV

# MACEDONIAN STORIES ABOUT PHILIP AND ALEXANDER

authorHOUSE®

AuthorHouse™
1663 Liberty Drive
Bloomington, IN 47403
www.authorhouse.com
Phone: 1-800-839-8640

Published by AuthorHouse    12/05/2012

ISBN: 978-1-4772-3924-7 (sc)
ISBN: 978-1-4772-3925-4 (e)

Dedicated to my children Filan, Zara and Ahil

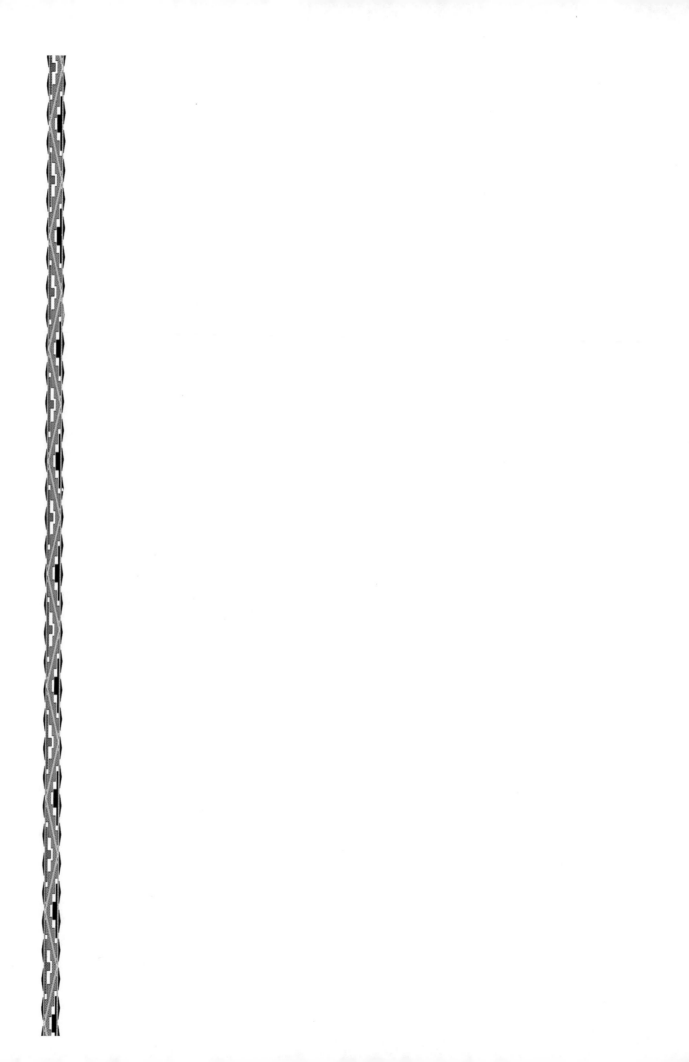

The number 8 is the symbol of eternity.
As there are two parts to the number eight, so there
are four stories each about Philip and about Alexander
They have made Macedonia eternal.
MAY THEIR MEMORY LIVE!

*The author dissociates himself from any local-political or historical interpretations. These stories are a personal view of the Macedonian Kingdom of 2500 years ago.*

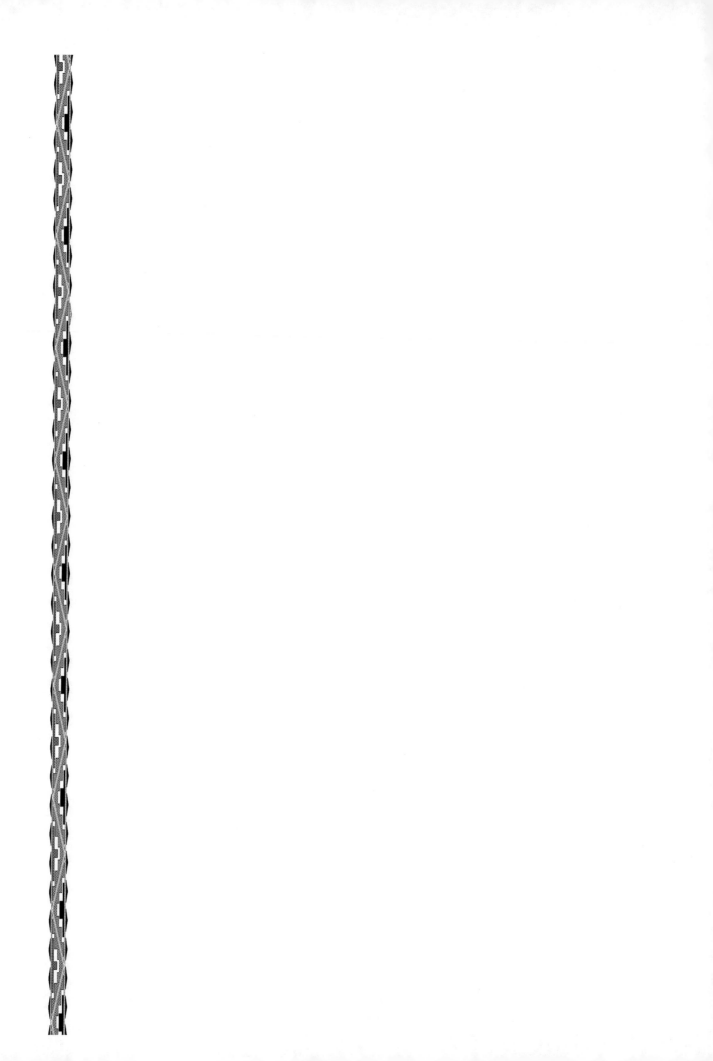

From the Author

It all began, the idea was conceived, when I moved away from Macedonia.

As time went by, various real situations in life fed and developed the embryo.

When I returned to Macedonia, it was already weighing down on me.

And the more I postponed it, the stronger the pressure became.

Feeling very fearful, I started to write these stories. My reason was warning me: 'You're not on your own ground. You will be seen as frivolous, unfit...ridiculous!

My heart was saying: You have no alternative. Write! That's how it is and there's no turning your back on it!

The struggle lasted for years.

I realized I was like a woman with child who has to give birth.

I only hope that this will be 'milk' for Macedonian children big and small....

Contents

## STORIES ABOUT PHILIP

## STORIES ABOUT ALEXANDER

# 4 STORIES ABOUT PHILIP

## THE POWER OF THE ORO

In olden times, the mighty state of Macedonia was known far and wide for its sound organization, and its people for their fine music and songs, and especially for their beautiful traditional dances, called oros.

At that time Persia was the greatest power and the most developed state in the known world. But even the Persians lauded the songs and dances of the Macedonians. These songs and dances were part and parcel of their everyday life. People danced and sang at weddings and festivals, and also when they were sad, for there were songs and dances for mourning and death as well. The dances were remarkably varied. Some in a quick rhythm, some slower... The songs and dances were adjusted to suit each specific event. No matter how well or poorly educated were the people, at a given time each and every one could sing the songs by heart and knew the steps of the dances. Those were times when a knowledge of what dances and songs were proper for what occasions was inherent to all.

Even the children, from the upper as well as from the lower classes, were taught Macedonian songs and dances very early in their lives, still toddlers, so to say. Life without the mastery of dancing and singing was simply inconceivable. Almost all, from the commonest people to the

King, were good dancers of the oro. The dancing style depended on the rhythm, and the steps were customarily five forward, ten back, ten forward, six back… Different oros had different rhythms. But some were so complex it required genuine dexterity to master them.

At a certain time, Macedonia fell into a grave crisis. The cities started to argue among themselves. Each ruler and prince wanted to be independent and to have his own kingdom. Chaos and unruliness held sway all around, and the people were falling out with each other. All this significantly damaged the economic power of the state.

But when the wise King came to the throne, he quickly became the most renowned King, for he managed to unite the Macedonians. What with good policies, what with his artfulness, he helped them to overcome their disputes. Region by region, they were reconciled and united. And the King told them about a great vision of his, to build an army that would be strong and powerful enough to conquer Persia, and from there

the world at large. Impossible as this vision may have sounded, the people, seeing that the young King was intent upon it, gave him their trust.

He also studied the enemy's tactics. In his childhood he had spent some time among the opponents in South Macedonia, who at that time had a famous and strong infantry. It was then and there that he started to harbour ideas about how to make the Macedonian army the strongest.

So when he ascended to the throne, he set about making his ideas come true. He created the phalanx and introduced new kinds of weapons, as well as light but strong shields and long spears. And he did not forget to better the soldiers' living conditions.

Moreover, he introduced protection, with improved helmets, lighter but harder, and better footwear and sandals. He went as far as to take part personally in making the equipment for his army, instructing the craftsmen who were manufacturing the clothes and the weapons. And he was the first to try out the new equipment on himself.

And he trained in full gear along with his soldiers. The army adored him, because he was always with them, and in the first line of infantry in the battles they fought. Right there where it was hardest, where until then there commonly stood either mercenaries or the lowest in society, thieves, hoodlums…

The King in the first rank of the infantry… this gave rise to tremendous euphoria. Every single soldier was ready to give his life for him.

But the start of drilling the Macedonian phalanx brought him deep disappointment. It was simply impossible to harmonise the soldiers' movements, because their spears were too long. And their lines were much too long as well, extending to infinity.

In the time needed for an order to reach from one end of the phalanx to the other (for the soldiers to turn left or right, for example) a great commotion was created that made it impossible to coordinate the army. In the beginning, drills were carried out for special units, smaller in number, but if coordination of the excellently trained special forces armed with their long spears was difficult, what was it going to be like on the battlefield, with thousands of soldiers lined one next to another and one behind another?

His dream, his vision of building an invincible infantry, started to crumble, and he himself was beginning to harbour doubts.

The young King was deeply disheartened, because he had invested so much effort, made so many plans and designs on how to train the soldiers to move in unison in battle. For the entire army to act with one accord. For all to be facing in the same direction at the same time and from the same position. The strength of the infantry lay in its orchestrated movement. It was imperative that all the soldiers moved in a given direction at the same moment.

The King despaired. Time flew. He was thinking, and thinking hard, but could not find a solution.

One day, a close associate of his invited the King to a wedding party. The King was in no mood to go, for he was making plans for great campaigns of conquest, and the thought that he would not be successful because he could not find a way to attune the infantry with the command and leadership was torturing him.

He felt discouraged, weak, lifeless. Fooled by his own vision of creating an invincible infantry with which the Macedonian army would conquer the world.

Heavy hearted and lost in thought he went to the wedding. The songs resounded and as at any wedding people were drinking wine and dancing the oro. Suddenly, the King's eyes shone with happiness, and he stood

up and joined the oro to dance with the others. His mood suddenly changed. Now he was very merry and filled with joy. The King danced as never before. He was thrilled by the dances. Perfection of movement. Total synchronisation. That was the movement for his phalanx.  All simultaneously to one side, forward… back.

His sudden happiness puzzled all those watching the King dance.

Every single man, from the first to the last in the long human chain dancing the oro, moved in such unison and so flawlessly that, simultaneously and without anyone giving the command, their feet trod left and right in perfect harmony.

The next morning, the King retreated to his chambers and drew the arrangements of the army on paper, with each change of battle position indicated not by orders, but by the names of different dances.

The following day the soldiers were practicing as a phalanx turning in a circle, attacking and retreating… He explained to them that, to a man, they were to dance the oro he told them to dance. They immediately understood the essence of the idea. From that moment on, commands were performed with ease.

In the battles that followed, the King would simply state the name of the dance and the mighty phalanx, in perfect arrangement, with huge spears and large shields, would start moving as one, to the millimetre. In perfect harmony and with incredible precision. Like a giant titan of unseen strength.

Thus, relying on his natural instinct and the power of the oro, the Macedonian King succeeded in creating an invincible army that people have been recounting stories about to this day.

## THE MIND REIGNS

Once upon a time there was a great Macedonian King whose strength and valour won him fame throughout the world. He was said to be a great military leader, but also very cruel, wild and merciless. There was, however, a small circle of people, those closest to him, who knew that their King was very wise. He always aspired to make good his intentions by means of negotiation, to avoid war and yet achieve his goal. And he intended much and had a grand goal – he wanted Macedonia to conquer the entire world.

At that time, however, there were various disturbances and disputes in his kingdom among the local and regional rulers. They were all on bad terms with each other. Each one against all others. Everyone against everyone. Brother and brother at each others' throats.

To overcome this problem, the King embarked on an action. He sent his emissaries to each of the quarrelling princes with a message – that the King gave his wholehearted support to him alone. Upon receiving this message, the princes strained their relations with their rivals even further. Misunderstandings escalated to such a degree that they start-

ed preparing to settle their accounts, as soon as possible, and slaughter each other in wars. And that was the moment the King was waiting for.

When they were all ready to go to battle, to kill each other to the last man, the King started visiting them one by one, appearing before them unannounced. He had with him his complete retinue and his troops armed to the teeth. All the princes were taken aback by his unexpected visits. The King pretended not to know anything about what was going on in the princedoms. "We had military manouevres nearby, so I thought I'd visit you…" he would say. "To rest at my best friend's…"

And soon the prince he was visiting, flattered by this great honour, would speak completely openly before the king and tell him all about the problems with the prince in the adjacent princedom and what he was preparing for… Because each of them believed that it was himself that the King supported, and so they hoped that the King's army would come to their help. But then the King ordered that the two antagonistic princes come before him with their armies. And once they stood before him he asked them for every one to hear: "What will you achieve by murdering those who are closest to you?"

The princes were dumbfounded.

"You will die an inglorious death, you will impoverish your families, increase even further your hatred for each other, and you will no longer trade with each other…" the King would continue. "You won't marry among yourselves, there will be no more of those wonderful wedding parties with dances and wine, no more of the contests between the young men of your two cities…"

They said nothing.

"Is there a man among you who will tell me what you will gain if you fight each other?"

Thus the King spoke at the top of his voice to the armies standing in ranks in front of him. All were silent, with their heads down, realizing the foolishness of what they had been about to do. The princes

too stood with lowered heads. But their hearts were filled with gratitude and love for the King, for having come at the right moment to help them.

And he did the same in all the belligerent princedoms.

Once the King had informed them about his own plans, they forgot all about their quarrels. Every man, to the very last, realized the absurdity of the situation their princes had put them in, and at the same time they were overwhelmed by the greatness of their King's ideas. The armies and the princes shook hands, and the King's visits ended in great celebration and merriment.

Thus, without spilling a drop of blood, the wise King managed to unite all the princes in Macedonia who had been each others' deadly foes. And thus he achieved great economic progress for the kingdom as a whole and

gained even greater respect for himself, as well as a strong, united army.

At that time there lived in the empire certain smaller groups of people, whose language the Macedonians could not understand. To them, their speech sounded like "creak" and they started calling them thus. But the 'creaks', or 'grchi' in the language of the Macedonians, were exceptional merchants who brought the people plentiful goods from all four corners of the world, and especially of the kind that could not be found in the kingdom.

The country abounded in good farm produce and livestock, handicrafts and other products, so the princedoms were trading among themselves to the benefit of all. And thus they lived in untroubled harmony.

However, those groups of people acquired a great deal of gold through trade, for in the land of

the Macedonians there was considerable demand for the products they supplied. And the gold they received from the Macedonians for certain luxury goods brought from afar was worth much more than the actual value of those goods. In time, as their economic strength grew, they started to think of themselves as being more civilized, and to group themselves into small towns enclosed by high walls.

But they were not arrogant only towards the Macedonians. In their greed for gold, they started to fight even among themselves. Each city waged war against some other of their cities, so that eventually they became a problem for the kingdom as a whole, for they stopped paying taxes to the Macedonian King.

All this troubled the wise King, so he decided to bring them under control. His army was now united and very strong. With the power vested in him he could, if he wished, annihilate them in a single day. But that was not his nature. He simply wanted to win them over to his side. He did not want to kill them, but to reconcile them and keep them as part of his kingdom. So that they would pay their taxes and work in the future as they always had done until then. Carrying on their trade, but recognizing the authority of the King as well.

But that small, wayward people had grown too smug, arrogant and impudent, and refused to obey his authority. Therefore, the wise King made a plan to conquer the cities one by one. He summoned his generals and shared his plan with them.

First, to besiege the town of the traders using the entire army, infantry and the cavalry, all armed to the teeth… to bring all the catapults and other horrendous military contrivances. Then subject the soldiers to vigorous and intensive daily drills, as if they were to fight in the most decisive and brutal battle. As if they were to fight the strongest enemy ever. Prepare the army for the fiercest attack ever launched. . . And when everything was ready, to send a messenger with a fully laden donkey to deliver an ultimatum. And the ultimatum was to say that if they surrendered and accepted the authority of the King, nothing would happen to them, no one would be punished and no houses would be set on fire. If not, the city would be levelled to the ground and all would be killed without mercy.

The generals found this plan very logical. But they could not but wonder about one thing.

"Why the fully laden donkey?" they asked. "And loaded with what?"

Now the King found their question absurd.

"What do you mean – with what? Well, if it's gold they crave most then we shall give them gold…" he told them, and then explained further: "How can you negotiate with an enemy if you don't offer him first that which he wants most? Later, once we've subdued them, they'll pay us back a hundredfold in taxes."

So they proceeded according to his plan. The donkey in front of the enemy's gates, with saddlebags filled with gold, proved to be a most powerful soldier. Frightened by the sight of the army preparing for attack, the people were confused and surprised to see a messenger before their gates. And when they opened the gates to let him in and saw that the donkey was loaded with gold, they breathed a sigh of relief and started

negotiating. And immediately some of them declared that the Macedonians and their King were not barbarians who killed and destroyed everything in their way, but had come to offer cooperation.

By such a strategy, the Macedonian King seized all their towns. And finally he came to the merchants' principal city. It was the biggest city and its citizens considered themselves special, the most learned of all. And therefore they were the most arrogant, and held the Macedonians in contempt. And they did not hesitate to show it, even belittling the King by calling him – a barbarian.

But the wise commander employed the same strategy. First he stationed his great army in front of the city walls. Then he sent a messenger with the threats, also leading two donkeys carrying loads of gold... This time, however, the tactic did not work. The citizens did not accept the loads. He sent them new, more frightening threats, and this time he gave the messenger four donkeys loaded with gold... Still nothing. He could not win them over. And he tried again with new and even more frightening threats, and with six donkeys laden with gold... Nothing helped. In the end, all attempts proved unsuccessful.

Then the King became seriously concerned. He knew he should bribe the merchants with something more than what he already offered, but what could that be? The King was thinking, searching for a solution, but nothing came to his mind. A day passed, then another… He was becoming visibly anxious, and his anxiety spread to his generals and eventually to the army. Some of the generals proposed that they should attack with all force and level the city to the ground, which was indeed logical, since they had surrounded the city with their huge army. Others proposed they should go back to Macedonia since this city was of no importance or significance to them and in any case the merchants would have to trade with them.

A few more days passed. The dilemma in the Macedonian army had already turned into open dispute. The King was uncertain what to do, and this led to heightened tension.

If he struck with force, he would trample over them and destroy them in the blink of an eye, but that would serve to confirm that they were right in calling him a 'barbarian'. If he let them be and returned to Macedonia, their arrogance and effrontery towards the Macedonians would only strengthen. He wanted to defeat them, but in a different way. How?

At a meal with his generals, two of his guests got into such a fierce quarrel that they left the table and went out in protest, one to one side, the other to the other.

Seeing this, the Macedonian King suddenly jumped from his seat and cried out loud: "I know how we shall conquer them!"

The massive army was deployed in front of the gates of the fortified city, with all their horses and cattle and all the spoils and trophies taken from the other battles. The King summoned the generals, who were overjoyed that they would finally make real their threats to the disobedient, trample them down and conquer them. But instead of giving them the order to attack, the King told them his new plan.

And this is what ensued:

He ordered that his army be divided into two camps and the soldiers train in fierce fighting with each other, and he told them in detail what to do.

The merchants carefully followed everything that was happening in front of their walls. They saw the army in the distance dividing into two camps and starting to fight each other, to shout at each other, with horses

galloping this way and that. Great confusion ensued, soldiers were falling dead on all sides. The struggle, the cries, the wailing, the thudding and neighing of the horses, went on all that day and night. In the morning, the little that was left of one group of the army stood on one side, with the even smaller remaining force of the other group on the other. Left there, in the broad plain in front of the city gates and before the merchants' hungry eyes, lay all that the original army had been carrying. The horses, the cattle, the tents, the trophies of war, everything they had. And amidst it all stood the six donkeys carrying the saddlebags of gold. The battlefield was strewn with dead bodies. Seeing this, the citizens opened wide the city gates and ran to the loaded donkeys and all that had been left by the army.

The minute the gates opened and the people ran out to snatch the plunder, the men left lying there, the 'dead' Macedonian soldiers, suddenly came to life, jumped to their feet, stormed into the city and conquered it.

Thus the King managed to conquer the greatest city of his opponents, losing not a single soldier. To this day, those who 'creek' when they speak cannot get over what the Macedonians did to them.

## THE BEST ALLY

In ancient times there lived, as we already know, the great Macedonian King who was not only strong, but also very wise. He prepared meticulously for every undertaking, and as commander of the army he studied his enemy carefully before going to battle. The enemy's numbers, ways and customs, then the location where the battle was to take place as well… He drummed it into his generals: "Never underestimate any enemy!"

The King always found some clever, unpredictable manoeuver that would so confuse the adversary that the Macedonian army would win the battle without incurring too many casualties. This is why he never lost a battle in any of the wars he waged. Everyone marvelled at his almost impossible achievements, and the news of his wisdom as a commander spread throughout the world. And the whole world was fascinated by his winning every single battle without a problem!

Many stories were told about him, some were even made up and certain supernatural and superhuman characteristics were ascribed to him. Some said he had entered into a pact with God, others that he used

magic... people were simply trying to explain what defied explanation, but one thing was clear to all – he was an extremely clever King.

As his youngest son grew up he manifested a growing interest in what his father did. And he was always at his father's heels.

When he was still very young, at the age of fourteen or so, his father had started taking him along and revealing to him the secrets he had learned, telling his son: "Even the strongest enemy has a particular weakness... But you have to look for it, while respecting his strength... Sometimes, the enemy's greatest strength can prove to be his greatest weakness as well... That's how you can defeat even the most mighty and unconquerable enemy..."

The young prince listened carefully, but he was still too young and inexperienced to understand the essence of what his father was telling him.

At that time, on the other side of the known world, in the farthest and mightiest empire of Persia, there was another King who had heard of the wise and invincible Macedonian conqueror and warrior. The stories that spread even in his own kingdom vexed him considerably, since it was he who had been considered the most powerful and indomitable warrior in the entire world. He was known for his numerous cavalry and their remarkably swift and well trained Arab horses. And so, after thorough preparations, he decided to gather his numerous infantry and cavalry and embark on a long journey, crossing many rivers and mountains to reach Macedonia and engage in battle with that invincible Macedonian King.

The news of the vast approaching army, fitted out with impressive weapons, war chariots, swift footed horses and a knowledge of all possi-

ble military techniques and technology known at that time, had already reached Macedonia.

Anxious generals gathered and informed the King about the approaching enemy. But their voices were tinged with fear. The King heard them out, gave them a long, serene look and said: "Well, my soldiers, this only goes to prove that we are strong and powerful… We shall deal with them just as we have dealt with all the others so far."

They were amazed that the King, having heard how strong and well-prepared the army of the enemy was, never even batted an eye.

And when the enemy's scouts came to negotiate the site for the battle with the great army, the King's youngest son was at his side. The young prince stood stupefied. It was the first time he had seen such strange soldiers, dark complexioned, with thin straight beards, mounted on such beautiful and powerful black horses. They wore unfamiliar clothes, bore curved sabers and wore turbans instead of helmets on their heads. Beside himself with agitation, he asked his father: "Father, how can our army win?" And his father replied: "You know son, if you have the sun as an ally, you will always win…"

The young prince did not understand his father at the time, but followed him to see where and how he would station the army. The battle was to be fought in the Pelagonia Valley near Heraclea, the city the King had built in honour of the great hero Heracles.

On that broad, flat plain, a vast expanse, the King was to decide on the position from which to fight the battle. He paced the area this way and that, spending almost the entire day there, and eventually reached a low lying area with a swamp, stones, and rough, difficult ground. He turned to his son and said: "Son, this is where I'm going to station my army… Here…"

The young prince was struck with amazement at the strangeness of this decision: of all that flat valley and of all the favourable places where they could station their army, his father had chosen the worst, one with rocks, water, mud and reeds. . . In short, he had chosen the most inappropriate ground. The prince was still young and unable to fully understand his father's reasoning.

Next they were joined by the generals, to whom the King presented his plan. He said, "My generals, the most important thing now, just as before each of the battles we've fought in the past, is to prepare the army by having all their shields painted gold and polished as if for a grand parade… And each shield must have special crystals set in the centre, to reflect the light like a hundred mirrors…"

The great military leader spoke on and on with great enthusiasm about the shields alone. Then he explained his tactics and the technology of the action which was based, in fact, on the polished shields. The generals started to whisper among themselves and to exchange looks full of fear and distrust.

The young prince was there all the time, never taking his bright, wary eyes off the generals, watching and following what they were saying. He asked: "Father, why are the generals so upset? And they're whispering to each other and mumbling… Perhaps they can't hear what you're saying?"

The King did not reply, but continued to talk about the shields. When he had finished, he simply informed them of the positions where the infantry and other units would be stationed.

As was the custom, the generals waited to the end to ask any questions that would help them understand the overall strategy better. As soon as the King gave the sign, they started shouting as one man. Then one of them expounded their doubts to the King, "Your majesty, we have always listened to you and done as ordered by you, and it's true we have always been victorious. But this time we are faced with a particularly mighty foe with the best possible military training and coming with a vast army… They are foreigners we have never engaged with in battle before, and they're said to be the strongest in the world… They have a huge cavalry and many war chariots and frankly, knowing all that, we can't make sense of your strategy…"

The King simply listened. Then another general took over: "Before every battle you tell us that the shields are most important. Today you've talked for over an hour about polishing our shields… As if we were going on parade… And finally, we don't understand why we should deploy our strongest infantry in this broad, flat valley, where we could station our cavalry and war chariots. But you intend to do exactly that, you'll station the army right here, on this rough and marshy ground where you can hardly walk on foot!"

The King watched them calmly and listened to their comments, and when each of them had had his say, he summed up their complaints that all amounted to one and the same issue – why this ground and why the highly polished shields?

Having expressed their objections, the generals fell silent and the King asked them: "Tell me, my friends, my most faithful generals, have I ever willingly exposed you to danger?"

They stood in total silence… He continued: "Is my goal not the same as yours, to win victory over our strongest enemy? And have you not understood by now that the Macedonian army has one great ally, the most powerful ally – the sun?"

Still silent, the generals stared at their King as he went on: "At nine or ten in the morning, when the enemy's cavalry is going to carry out their fiercest attack, we shall be in this position…

"The sun will shine strongly in our faces and our eyes, but also on our shields. The reflection from the shields will be like a hundred glaring

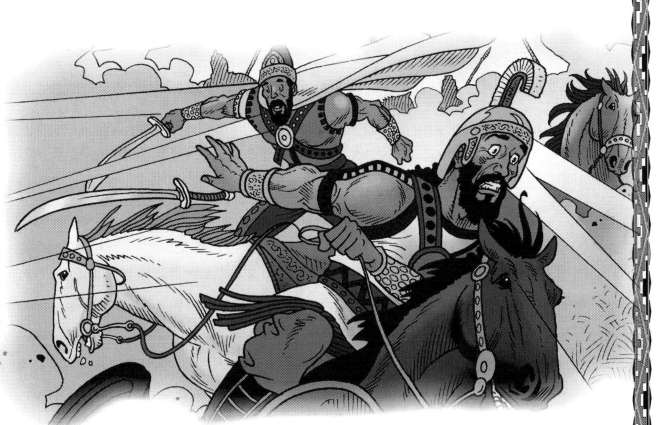

suns, and we shall be able to direct it straight into the eyes of the horses, virtually if not literally blinding them… They won't know which way to run… Galloping towards us over this vast plain, they will start to lose their formation, disoriented by the strong sunlight. And we shall have the rough, marshy ground behind us. I know the army will have no-where to retreat, but will have to move bravely forward…"

The generals listen to all this and it sounded impossible, but then they remembered the many battles in the past when the King had put them in positions they were not even aware of. But now, he was telling it openly for the first time, explaining the reason for all the previous victories in their battles.

When the battle started, the entire infantry of the Macedonian King was lined up in a single row with perfectly polished mirrorlike shields in front of them. When the enemy's cavalry charged in a fierce attack, the ground shook from the horses' heavy hooves. The sun shone strongly, as if it knew this was going to be a horrendous battle in which its help was needed. And so, with its light mirrored back from

the shields of the Macedonian infantry, it shone into the eyes of the enemy's horses – a light as strong as the light of hundred suns. After only a dozen metres of charging at full gallop, the horses began to lose their orientation. And as they dashed about in the field, on the flat ground left at the disposal of the enemy, they created havoc in their ranks. This shattered the shock section, so they could not reach the Macedonian army. They were completely disoriented and in utter chaos. And that was all the Macedonian infantry was waiting for to storm deep into the enemy's lines and crush them. With the ingenious technique of the sun's reflected light, the adversary's greatest strength was turned into its greatest weakness, and their army was trampled down by the Macedonian King.

Watching from a safe distance as his father crushed the mightiest army with ease, the youngest son of the King, eyes wide open, mouth gaping, and heaving with excitement, understood his father's words and the wisdom of his saying, that he who has the sun as an ally – shall never lose a battle!

# THE GREATEST SACRIFICE

A vast and powerful army embarked on a campaign of conquest and seized almost the entire world as it was then known to humanity. Macedonia was next in their path. It too was attacked.

The King had three sons, and the eldest was always with him. He was born to be a soldier. Strong and bright, courageous and fearless. He loved his two younger brothers very much. Particularly the youngest, the one who wanted to know everything. The two often practiced wrestling, and he showed his brother various tricks and moves in martial arts. Whenever possible, the youngest prince hung around him and his weapons, endlessly asking questions about various battles and listening openmouthed to the stories he old him. He looked up to his eldest brother as to an unattainable idol…

Everyone believed that the eldest son would be the true successor to the throne. The King was very proud of him. But he was also very strict with him. He wanted his son to develop fully before he came to the throne intended for him. The soldiers held the King's son in high regard, because when he was with them he was a common soldier and that was how he acted. But in battle, he became a lion and everyone wanted to be near him.

Persia embarked on the conquest of Macedonia. The Macedonians were losing battles. Battle after battle, on all sides. The King was furious with everyone. He raved at them all, imposed severe punishments on the disobedient, kept replacing generals… But still new battles were lost. The army grew frightened of the enemy's strength. The generals, his most loyal friends, were powerless and confounded. They could not believe their eyes, seeing their King helpless, ranting and raging. The King was mad as a hornet. He lost trust in everybody, saw traitors in all. He punished even the smallest mistakes he believed his subjects had made severely and mercilessly. Punishment left and right… But he was still losing battles. The army's morale was declining.

And the Macedonian people as a whole were desperate. Day after day the enemy was taking over an ever larger part of their homeland. In the face of such a mighty army the soldiers' fighting spirit dropped very low.

The King wanted to increase his army, so the Macedonian soldiers who were in charge of the horses, kitchen and food supplies were replaced with mercenaries, who did not understand their language. But they were the kind of people who would do anything for a piece of gold, even though they did not like the Macedonians. And this did not help, either.

In one very fierce battle both sides suffered great losses and captured many prisoners. The Macedonians managed to take one of the enemy's most important generals prisoner. However, the King's son was also captured in that battle.

A truce was agreed. The Persians wanted their general back at any cost. He was a great strategist and it was he who led in all their victories and conquests. He was indispensable to the Persian army. The Macedonians became aware of this fact as soon as they started negotiating his possible release.

The enemy offered piles of gold and other precious riches for his release. The King hoped that the ransom gold would help him pay many mercenaries whom he could then use to stop the enemy's advance, and at the same time lessen the loss of Macedonian soldiers.

But word that the King's eldest son was among the captives taken by the enemy soon spread in the ranks of the two armies. The enemy applied the cruellest possible methods on the Macedonian soldiers to find out which was the King's son. They tortured them and beat them, but they said nothing. And the enemy had to be careful not to torture anyone to death, for fear it might be the King's son. Eventually they exhausted all their harshest means of torture, and still no one had pointed out the King's son. The enemy were amazed by the loyalty, faithfulness and strength of the Macedonian soldiers. And when they thought that there was no way of finding the prince, they declared that all the captives were going to be murdered. The Macedonian army heard of this and they knew that if it happened the King's son would be murdered too. And then the enemy's so highly prized and indispensable general would be killed by the Macedonian King.

In this situation, while the wisest Persians were deliberating what to do next, how to find a way out of this dire position, a mercenary from the Macedonian army who was in charge of the horses came to them. As a non Macedonian he did not hesitate to ask bluntly and arrogantly for a pot of gold as a reward for revealing the King's son to them.

At that moment everything changed. Now the negotiations would be much easier and the Persians were certain that they would be successful, for they held the Macedonian King's son captive.

Soon every one in the army knew that the King's son had been betrayed by a mercenary for a pot of gold. And they were sure the King would return the enemy's mightiest general. The situation was worse than ever. No one believed any longer that it was possible to defend the homeland. The fighting spirit hit bottom. The King found himself in a most difficult position. His son, his successor, his pride, was in enemy hands. He despaired. Feeling utterly powerless, he decided that it would be too hard to live on, and saw death as a merciful reward. He wanted to set out and free his son himself... but it would be a useless death, and

then they'd kill his other sons as well... and all the soldiers... they'd occupy and destroy his land... and that would be the end of everything...

Never before had the King known such a state of mind. Deep down he had always believed he had the solution to any problem.... And now he had to face the fact that this was not so!

The enemy's negotiators arrived. It was a meeting of the highest military officials of both sides, at which all agreed that the proposal was acceptable. To exchange the high general for the King's son. All eyes were now on the King. A long moment of dead silence.

The King was speechless. It was as if he had heard his death sentence... And not only his, but the death sentence for Macedonia...

And then something burst forth from him. Something no one, not even he himself, expected. It gushed out from the depths of his heart. First he whispered something... Then said it aloud... And then shouted it at the top of his voice...

"I will not exchange a general for a soldier! No exchange of a general for a soldier!"

The silence that followed was even deeper then before.

Nobody knew how long it lasted. All those present were stunned. After a while, the enemy's delegation prepared to leave. They could hardly stand on their feet. They staggered as if about to fall at any moment. A strange feeling of defeat overwhelmed them….

The Macedonian delegation still did not move. The King's words were resonating like an echo in their heads. At the same time they felt as if thousands of ants were crawling up their bodies. An unknown sensation that felt as if a huge invisible force was filling their bodies, tightening their muscles, . . fists… jaws. In such a state of mind and body they only managed to hear the angry voice of their King – ordering that the entire army be readied for tomorrow's attack.

The Persian King was shocked by the sight of his envoys when they returned to the encampment. "Why are you so downcast?" He asked. "What has happened, that you look so defeated?"

And they told him about the negotiations with the Macedonians.

That was an even greater shock for the Persian King. He summoned all his generals. "We've encountered a fearless and invincible enemy. The Macedonian King is a man whom I would like to have as a friend, not one that I wage war with," he said. "Never before have I seen such courage and love for one's country".

But there was no time to reverse decisions.

The battle was set for the next morning.

The Macedonian King was in the first rank, in the first line of the infantry. He charged forward valiantly. His generals and all his army were right behind him, following him closely. They fought superhumanly, as if they had some invisible force around them that enabled them, with ease and superiority, to defeat what only the day before had been the invincible enemy.

Faced with such a violent attack, the Persians army soon fell into disarray. The soldiers started to flee, running away in all directions, wherever they could. They were running for their lives. But the Macedonians were everywhere, catching up with them… and had no mercy for any-

one. They pursued them for days … for weeks. The King, and all who followed him, did not sleep, never stopped nor ate… never washed their faces. They were a terrifying sight. And the enemy was terrified. The Macedonians created panic in Persia. They chased the enemy all the way to Palestine, and not an enemy soldier survived. When they reached the Jordan they stopped to water the horses. Here and now, to a man, all fell to the ground exhausted.

They slept like the dead.  It is said that they slept for days. And then, when the soldiers started washing the weeks old dried blood from their bodies, it was as if they were waking up from the trance they had been in all that time. The turquoise blue water turned red. They slowly became aware of everything that had happened and started to call out the name of the King, to praise him, to remember the events. It all turned into a great celebration. People now liberated from Persian rule were joining them from all sides, bringing copious gifts, food and wine… They all bowed to the Macedonians.

The King entered the river to wash himself. He was the last to go in. He could not manage on his own, and was aided by his most faithful friends. His generals. They washed him for hours. The blood of the enemy mixed with the dust and dried by the fierce sun seemed to have become a strong protective armour. An armour that protected him from the terrible oncoming pain. And now, in the water, it was as if they were removing the most healing ointment for his wound. He began to feel the pain growing in his muscles, in his chest, in his soul. Only now did he understand what he had done… what had happened…

He felt he would not be able to survive the approaching wave of pain. But although present, the pain did not strike… Strangely, he was calm. But he felt as if he had a sword stuck through the centre of his chest. A constant sensation. He was unable to breathe in or out properly…

The Palestinians gathered on the bank watched all this. And wondered at the sight of the terrifying soldiers, real monsters that entered the water to come out as handsome white men. From that time on the people considered the river Jordan a holy river.

Everything around the King was so very different from how he himself felt. The people celebrated him, bowed to him, carried him on their shoulders. Their eyes glistened when they described the heroic exploits of their King… But nobody mentioned his son.

He answered their greetings, smiled, returned his generals' hugs... took part in the celebrations. But the sensation in his chest never subsided.

The people were euphoric. The generals wanted to continue the campaign. To conquer all of Persia. But the King said, "I have done enough here... we are returning to Macedonia".

On the way home the celebration of the King's exploits was constantly growing. The greatest festivity took place in Macedonia. No Macedonian King before him had been welcomed like this. He and his army passed through a tunnel of people, young and old. All there to honour him. They showered him with flowers, and bagpipes, shawms and drums echoed on all sides. People were dancing the oro...

The only person who did not come out to greet him was his wife. She alone continued to cry and mourn for their son.

When the King appeared at the door, she threw herself at him like a wounded lioness. He stood unmoving like a marble statue. And she cursed him, called him son murderer, screamed... And had they not stopped her she would have stabbed him with the knife she had hidden in her robes. It was the last time they saw each other.

Several years passed. The glory of the King spread to all four corners of the world. For the people of Macedonia he was the liberator, the greatest commander. Qualities were ascribed to him that only gods were worthy to possess.

The sensation in his chest never changed. Nor did his wife's hatred for him. She was beside herself with grief. Obsessed by the thought of avenging her son. She could not, nor did she want to accept that making the sacrifice of him had saved them all, had saved Macedonia.

At the celebration of the King's birthday she bribed a non Macedonian with much gold, and he stabbed a knife into the King's bosom. Hitting the exact place where the King had felt the blade all those years. Stabbed, he felt relieved. He felt he could breathe again. But those were his last few breaths. His youngest son held him in his arms. He had grown into a strong young man.

"You look so much like your brother… Take up where I left off. Make Macedonia so great and powerful that no one can attack it ever again …" these were the King's last words.

And the youngest son kept the word he gave his father. He conquered all of Persia, became the King of Persia. To avenge his beloved brother, he burnt the magnificent capital to cinders. He conquered all the then known world and made Macedonia the greatest and mightiest kingdom of all times.

56

# 4 STORIES ABOUT ALEXANDER

# THE WILD HORSE

Once upon a time there lived a great and mighty Macedonian King who had three sons. The eldest was twenty, the middle one eighteen and the youngest twelve. When he returned from one of his successful campaigns during which he had freed many territories, the King was given the gift of a beautiful horse. The horse was strong and young, but very wild, for no one had tamed it.

When the horse was brought to the King's palace the court and the generals and everyone in the city gathered around him to admire its strength and beauty, and its untamability. Since no one had managed to stay on its back till then, the King jokingly proposed to his generals, soldiers and those closest to him: "Let's hold a contest tomorrow... He who manages to tame and bridle this horse shall be my heir and shall become King of Macedonia".

His words were taken seriously by all. And the whole city hurriedly began preparing for the contest for which the strongest and bravest young men of the kingdom entered their names. Among them were his two elder sons. The youngest was too young to be allowed to try his hand. He could only watch the competition.

As always, he hung around his elder brother, whom he looked up to as an unattainable idol. The man he himself wanted to be like one day.

The contestants gathered and the contest began, and one after the other the bravest and strongest attempted to bring the horse under control. But as soon as anyone mounted it, the horse would become so powerfully enraged that rearing left and right it threw them off one by one, often even before they had managed to mount it at all.

Then it came to the eldest son's turn. Being the strongest, and very proud, he considered himself the heir to his father's throne. Though known as a good rider, the King's son too was thrown by the horse and was hurt so badly that even his life was at risk.

The sight of the best rider among them being thrown off like a rag inspired an even greater fear of the infuriated wild horse in the other contestants. But on the other hand, both contestants and spectators felt somehow relieved and pleased that not only had the King's son failed to tame the horse, but the attempt had almost cost him his life. Seeing this,

the King's second born son and the others who had entered to ride the horse withdrew from the competition.

The eldest son took his failure with the horse very much to heart. When the horse was taken back to its enclosure he called the guards and ordered them angrily: "You're not to give it any food or water! Disobey, and I personally will cut off your heads! You won't give it food or water, so it'll become exhausted, and then I'll win at the next competition." The youngest brother was there again, somewhere near him.

Terrified by the threats of the king's eldest son, the guards decided to organize themselves thoroughly and keep a watchful eye on the untamable animal. And to be especially cautious with any unexpected visitors who might unwittingly violate the orders.

For the first few days the eldest son called at the stable every day to look at the horse and check whether the guards were obeying the orders he had given them.

He was pleased to see that after a few days spent in the hot sun without water or food the horse stood motionless in one spot and no longer neighed. He ordered the guards to keep it like that in the coming days, and did not visit any more.

The King's youngest son, however, was a child who wandered all over the place, including the stables and the horse as well, and watched it with curiosity for he too liked the horse very much. And when he heard his brother's threatening words he thought it was unfair, and said to himself: "Well, I won't allow it! How can anyone torture such a beautiful, graceful horse by depriving him of food and water in this heat?" There were many things he did not understand. But he began to see his brother in a different light.

While the guards sat guarding the horse, never expecting that the King's youngest son could do any harm, he gradually began to approach the horse and talk to him. But the exhaustion and hunger he could see

in the animal's eyes urged him to do something about it. And so every night he secretly sneaked into his father's cellar to fill a bucket with apples and a pail with water. He would quietly come to the enclosure where the wild horse stood. He called it with whispered words and offered it food and water.

The first day he did this the wild horse still refused to have any contact with a human being, and so it was with the King's youngest son as well. It was still wild and angry, and did not touch the food…

Another day passed. But after the fearsomely high temperature of the day, the horse gave in and started to drink the water. The following day it accepted an apple… And the day after, it ate all the apples and drank a whole pail of water.

The King's youngest son was overjoyed that the horse had started to eat and drink. And he continued the ritual, taking a bucket of apples and a pail of water to the horse every day. The horse showed the first signs of friendship and joy at seeing the little prince by swishing its tail. That was how it greeted the boy every time he approached it. After a few days the prince began to stroke its nose, and the horse peacefully ate the apples from the prince's outstretched hand.

The King's eldest son was confident that, left without food or drink in the extremely hot weather, the horse was slowly weakening and being worn down. When two weeks had passed, he went to his father to ask him to hold another competition to tame the wild horse. And at the same time he clearly stated his wish to be the first contestant. His father found it a little strange, but laughed and said: "Last time you were the last to mount him… And even though the contestants before you had tired the horse, it ended in disaster for you. How are you going to succeed as his first rider, now that he's well rested? But you have my consent… If you feel certain about this, we can organize the contest and you'll be the first contestant."

The news that there was to be a second competition and that the most successful contestant would be the King's successor spread with the speed of lightning through the city.

Thinking that the horse had been without food or water for several weeks, the King's eldest son was there to ride it first. He approached the

animal feeling very confident, his head held high, his step calm. He did not even look at the horse, he was so confident that he would mount the exhausted animal as one gets on the back of a stubborn donkey that refuses to move.

But… the moment he sat on the horse's back he felt that a powerful whirlwind had snatched him up. The horse reared in rage and leapt this way and that, not only freeing himself of the rider but throwing him over the fence. Once again the King's eldest son barely survived. The terrifying sight of the furious horse redouble the fear in the other contestants, and the King's question as to whether anyone else wanted to compete was meant simply as a joke.

The news had swiftly spread that although the horse had been deprived of food and water for weeks, it was still extremely strong and wild, so all the contestants withdrew from the competition.

Seeing what had happened, the King's youngest son approached his father and asked him: "Father, may I be allowed to try and mount the horse?"

His question rang like a bell in the sudden silence which immediately gave way to hilarity and hearty laughter, since no one could imagine any such thing. The crowd tried to dissuade him, to persuade him to withdraw his brave proposal to ride the wild horse when even the best riders had given up. But the little prince was adamant, so his father agreed and said to him: "All right son, if you're not afraid to ride it, you may try to do so."

The little prince approached the horse, which remained calm, instinctively feeling his affection. As he mounted the horse the crowd held their breath. The women even covered their eyes, expecting the horse to start leaping and bucking and to shake the rider off.

To their surprise, however, the horse began to run in a circle, decorously and with an extraordinarily light step. As if it wanted to show them all who its real master and rider was. Then everyone cheered: "This is a miracle! This is a real miracle! The youngest prince will be the King's heir!" And the young prince defiantly looked for the eldest brother in the dust.

And that is how it was. When he came of age, the youngest son ascended to the throne and became the most famous king of all times. And the horse remained his true and loyal friend and a faithful companion in all his campaigns and battles to the end of his life.

# THE FIRST BATTLE

In the olden days of the great Macedonian King and his three sons, this king became famous in the known world for his courage and also for his wisdom. He never suffered defeat in any of the battles that he fought.

He was adored by his youngest son, who wanted always to be with him, with his army, with the horses. To watch from a distance the battles his father led, to feel the tumult and the tension, and also the fear in the eyes of the people. Closely following the preparations for encounters, he was fascinated by the way in which his father planned the battles and, unlike other children, he seemed to feel no fear but rather was overwhelmed by a strange sensation of excitement.

As he grew he gained more and more understanding of the many things his father told him over the years, things he had heard many times but had not been ready to understand fully. One of the many things his father drummed into him was: "Remember that in battles the enemy's greatest strength may easily prove to be his greatest weakness… And also, my son, our greatest weakness can prove to be our greatest strength."

Try as he might he could not understand the true meaning of this maxim which his father reiterated so many times. As the years went by he found himself thinking about it more and more often. At times he even thought that maybe there was not real meaning to it at all, and that maybe his father was simply making fun of him. But deep in his young heart he felt that these words hid a great secret, that it was here that the key to his father's success lay. But how could he reach the essence of it?

At the age of eighteen he was already a handsome young prince and a very strong young man. But it needed a real battle with a real enemy to turn the boy into a man.

And that time came.

One day his father told him: "Son, you are going to lead the army in the next battle".

From that moment on the youngest prince seemed really to have grown up, feeling the importance and gravity of what he was faced with. And only then, for the first time in his life, did he experience a fear like no fear he had ever felt. He felt his stomach literally cramp with fright.

Ever since the King had announced that his youngest son would be at the head of the army in the battle that awaited them, the young prince had felt that all the soldiers, including the generals, had become uncertain, and seemed to watch him with fear in their eyes. He suspected they were all discussing him because any talk stopped the moment he appeared somewhere. He had the feeling they were pretending to his face, making it appear that they did not mind in the least that they would be led by no other than him in the battle. But he could sense their anxiety and fear whenever he stood before them.

The young prince noticed all this and took it very hard, deep down feeling his own anxiety as well.

When the horses and all the equipment were nearly ready, two days before the battle in which he was to lead the army, he went into the forest, to a place where he used to play alone when he was a child. There, memories of events from his childhood started to whirl in his head, scenes of the battles his father had orchestrated using various techniques. . . And in particular the brilliant tricks he used to outwit his enemies and achieve his far famed victories. The scenes of the great celebrations and parades following such victories flickered in his mind and made him tingle with excitement.

In his mind's eye he saw again the happy faces of the soldiers returning victorious from battle. And how they carried his father on their shoulders after a battle in which they had triumphed.

But he was also terrified by the very thought that if he failed in his first battle he wouldn't be able to face his friends, the girls, the common folk, nor meet the eyes of the soldiers he had led into defeat.

All this made him so anxious he could not even sit and rest, but kept walking on and on in the forest and thinking… Thinking about how to deal with his fear and responsibility.

And then he remembered his father's words about how his greatest weakness, his fear, might prove to be his greatest advantage.

He felt powerless, frightened and defeated in advance. As if he had no strength to face the responsibility ahead of him, as if he could not possibly come before his people, as if he could already see his defeat, and also everybody's sad eyes on him.

How could he possibly turn his weakness into an advantage?

As he walked through the forest, lost in thought, he heard the clatter of horses' hooves in the distance. And that thudding made by many horses seemed to be accompanied by the voices of a large crowd of people. Slightly taken aback, he stopped in his tracks. The thought crossed his mind: could his army have started without him? So he hurried toward the tumult. He was already running when he came to a clearing at the far end of which he saw a group of shepherds sitting and playing the bagpipes, pipes, shawms and drums …. Just a few men, yet so much noise that it could be heard from a great distance.

The closer he came to them the more clearly he recognized the rhythm of a Macedonian song in the beating of the drums which he had mistaken for the clatter of horses. As he walked towards the group he felt that the rhythm, the shrill sound of the shawms and bagpipes, made him more and more relaxed, as if dissipating his fear, filling him with joy and courage.

When he had almost reached the shepherds an idea suddenly flashed through his mind.

By then the shepherds had seen him and stopped playing to stand up and greet the King's youngest son. But he turned on his heel and started to run back as fast as he could. The shepherds were bewildered. They stood wondering what was the matter with the prince.

And he ran with all his strength to the soldiers who were making the final preparations before setting out. He headed straight for the headquarters. The soldiers were astonished to see the prince breathless with running, and their first thought was that something terrible must have happened.

When he entered the headquarters the generals jumped to their feet,

for they had never before seen the prince with his eyes glaring, out of breath… What on earth is this, what has happened to him now?

Then the young prince shouted: "I know we're going to win!"

This confidence in victory astonished them even more, for they knew he had no experience as a military leader.

The young prince ordered all the soldiers to get bagpipes, drums, shawms and pipes. His order dismayed the generals, who could not comprehend such madness. They even started to mock him. What's the prince thinking of, planning to go into battle against a powerful enemy with his own army carrying shawms and drums instead of weapons, as if they were going to a wedding?

But the soldiers recognized in his eyes that glimmer they always saw in his father's eyes when he had

an idea that no one could understand at first. The young prince was so elated by his idea that no one even thought of contradicting him. It was just before the very start, when the entire army was ready, fully equipped with horses, carriages, and all their military equipment, that he ordered the soldiers to line up. And he himself inspected every soldier in his enormous army to see that each of them really had a musical instrument with him. And the order to move was not given until he had checked the last of them.

Naturally, the King had learned about all this. His generals had come to tell him that his son was not experienced enough to lead the army. And that it would be a real disaster and that every one was mocking his orders, even now... What would happen when the battle began?

The King heard out his generals' objections patiently. Then he rose from his seat and looking them up and down told them with evident pride in his voice: "My friends, my faithful generals, just you listen to him… And I assure you, you will prove victorious! Believe in your victory…"

The generals left more confused than when they had come to their King.

And then came the time to set out. The soldiers lined up for the march. Mounted on his horse, the prince took his place at their head. He appeared not to be sitting but leaping in his saddle, as if he could hardly wait for the hour of this decisive battle to strike. Everyone's eyes were on him and every single man wondered where such courage had suddenly come to him from.

The following morning they were to fight a mighty enemy, far famed for military skill, modern weaponry and powerful cavalry. Led by a fa-

mous soldier who was an equal to their own King, not to this brat who didn't know what he was doing... So the generals thought, but they could not but obey.

The Macedonian army was obviously anxious, uncertain and frightened before the battle that awaited them in the morning. But all were struck by the sight of the young prince walking among them and radiating an extraordinary confidence, joy and courage. And he even talked with the generals and the soldiers, joked with them... Had they not known this was his first battle they would have thought they had some very experienced commander, but...

As darkness fell the soldiers were preparing to sleep, so as to be well rested before the battle the following day. But the prince ordered them to gather before him, and each man with his instrument, as well.... Again, his order created evident confusion among his men. Yet they had no choice but to obey.

When the whole vast army had gathered in one place, the prince ordered that each soldier start to play his own favourite melody on his instrument, or to start beating the drum. And he told them to do this until dawn, when they would go straight into battle, without any sleep...

And that is what they did.

When each of the thousands of soldiers started to play his own song or beat the drum, it created an unbelievable din and throbbing, which carried them all away. Entranced, they beat on the drums, danced and laughed... Their anxiety was long gone. The deafening noise, the rhythm and the music had filled them with an inexplicable excitement.

They could not wait to fall on the enemy.

On the other side, where the enemy's army was encamped, the soldiers had retired, planning to be rested for the battle ahead of them, but no one could sleep. The thunderous noise was heard only too well, so like the thunder of thousands and thousands of horses, the voices of a huge army...

As the night passed, the enemy army became more and more overwhelmed by panic. From what they could hear, the number of their op-

ponents must be colossal… So they assumed. Not only the soldiers, but the enemy generals as well, and even their leader, were bewildered by such a great noise of soldiers and horses… It must be huge, that force they were to fight tomorrow, they thought. That was their impression.

At the first attack by the Macedonian army led by their young prince the enemy was already in disarray, frightened and defeated. Seeing the first line of cavalry charging fearlessly, euphoric, yelling loudly at them, they dropped their weapons and started to flee…

And that was how the young prince won his first real victory in the spirit of his father. The enemy suffered a severe and crushing defeat, with minimal loss of life on the Macedonian side. From that day on musical instruments became an integral part of Macedonian military equipment.

The victory won, everyone began to celebrate. They took out their musical instruments again, and all started to play, but now in unison, one and the same song. The young prince's song. And it has resounded ever since from Macedonia and far distant places.

# THE GREATEST BATTLE

In olden times, in Macedonia, the still young but mighty King soon became famous as a great leader, and his exploits were the talk of the whole world. People admired him so much that they considered him as almost a god, not just an ordinary human being. At any time and in any place he was the one who found the appropriate answers and the right solutions to all the problems in his mighty kingdom.

Yet whenever he was faced with a particularly important decision, he remembered his father and asked himself the question: how would my father have dealt with this problem? Perhaps that is why he became so powerful, because he was not complacent.

Winning one great victory after another and gradually conquering the whole known world, the wise Macedonian King and his army reached as far as India. Now at that time India was considered to be at the end of the world.

On their long journey along distant routes, the Macedonian army saw many strange peoples and cultures, new customs, and food that smelled and tasted strange. The soldiers acquired enlightening firsthand experience. And yet they really thought that India was the end of the world, that there was nothing beyond that land.

In India they came across many strange animals as well. And the strangest of all was the elephant, which they saw then for the first time in their lives. They could not have imagined that such an animal existed, an animal so big and strong. They also marvelled at how the people used the elephants, for work donkeys were commonly used for in Macedonia. They served to carry burdens, to be ridden, and for various domestic purposes. It tickled the soldiers' fancy to think of the many different uses the Macedonian donkey could be put to if it was as big as this … But what would they do when that donkey became stubborn… How could they make it move from the spot if it was so gigantic…

When the Macedonia army entered the territory of India, word immediately spread that the land had been invaded by a foreign military leader who aimed to conquer it and become its king, thus accomplishing his goal of having all the known world under his rule.

The strength and courage of this army, as well as the feats of the Macedonian King, were already known in India. But the king of India and his people were not in the least frightened or worried. They felt confident that there was no living soul in this world who could defeat the imperial Indian army.

So all they did in India was simply to gather the army and the countless war elephants that were specially trained as killer elephants, with knives bound to their trunks and legs. The animals, trained and equipped for combat, had proved to be a lethal weapon in battles with any enemy. Many invaders had tried to conquer this vast land, greedy for its wealth, but all of them had failed. And they had failed because when the hour came for battle with the imperial army of India, the enemy was swiftly trampled underfoot and destroyed, thanks to the specially trained killer elephants.

When the time came to determine the field of battle, certain rumours reached the Macedonian army and various stories started to spread among the soldiers. The Macedonians were renowned as extraordinarily brave soldiers who dutifully obeyed their beloved leader, but this time they were taken aback and confused by a situation which was new to them. They had heard about the killer elephants, about how they were deployed in the front line of battle, armed with special sabres fixed to their trunks and legs, so that in comparison with them the Macedonian cavalry and their chargers looked like toys.

For the first time ever the Macedonian army felt fear. The generals gathered and started trying to persuade their King to withdraw from

the battle with the Indian army because they were obviously going to be defeated.

The Macedonian King could not accept their reasoning, even though after all his years of waging war he was now faced with a problem which at that moment seemed insurmountable. And yet he never wavered and never entertained the idea that he should withdraw his army. That, for him, would have been the greatest defeat and even greater shame.

But he was warned that there were many elephants, that the enemy's plan was to position them in the first line of battle, and that they literally trod down everything they encountered. The infantry would follow behind them and then the cavalry…

He did not know what to do, what strategy to employ or what steps to take. His generals kept urging him to withdraw.

In this desperate situation, he went to his tent, took off his sword, armour, helmet and military outfit and ordered: "Bring me some ragged clothes and a scarf. I'm going for a few days' walk to get familiar with the surroundings… I don't want any of the army to follow me, nor anyone to look for me…"

He changed his clothes and transformed himself into an Indian villager, with a turban on his head. He left in the company of just one experienced Indian to serve him as interpreter.

The generals were astounded by the King's decision, some even thought he had panicked and lost his mind. Various rumours relating to his conduct started circulating among the soldiers. Some said he had simply run away and left them in the lurch in the face of the Indian army. And the Macedonian troops' uncertainty and apprehension grew even stronger.

And the King, dressed like an Indian villager, set out on a journey through the local villages, far from his frightened soldiers and his equally scared generals. He hoped that if he was left to think in peace he would find a strategy for the battle which he simply refused to see as lost in advance.

As he walked on and on he thought back to the many battles behind him and the many seemingly hopeless situations where he had, nevertheless, always found a means of defeating the enemy. He remembered his early youth, and his father – the great Macedonian King, to whose throne he had succeeded. He who had solved all problems with such ease, managing to find the weak spot even in the mightiest enemy. Everyone has a weakness, a weak spot. Even the strongest army has its weakness. And even that which is their greatest strength can turn out to be their greatest weakness. That is what his father had taught him… He recalled his very words.

But even now, it still sounded mostly like mere talk… For he had encountered an insoluble problem, in the face of which even his invin-

cible father would probably have admitted defeat and withdrawn before the killer elephants. The Macedonian King knew all this very well and racked his brains over the problem, but still he could see no way out… His adversary was an enormous army, with such powerful animals the like of which he had never seen before, lined up next to one another and trained to kill everything in their path! How could one find the weak spot in such an army?

Lost in these thoughts he walked on, feeling as if he was on his last legs. Had he tripped and fallen he would hardly have found the strength to get up. That is how faint hearted he felt… Like once long ago, on the eve of his first battle… But he was practically a child then. And now he was the mightiest King in the world who felt so terribly powerless.

And so the Macedonian King roamed the villages as a beggar, and as he walked he looked around and thought. And he saw that there were a lot of livestock in this land, and especially cows. So he asked his interpreter: "Why do people keep so many cattle? Cows in particular?"

His companion then explained to the King the Indian tradition and the cult of the holy cow which is considered a 'sacred animal' and the greatest friend of human beings. Therefore, no one is allowed to kill a 'sacred animal', but they keep them until they die a natural death. And he also explained that the milk the cows give made it possible for the villagers to feed their large families, and the dairy products made from milk were traded for other products the owners of the cows did not have.

The everyday life, views and beliefs of the Indian villagers intrigued the King, and at the same time they distracted him from his troublesome thoughts. For the first time in his life he began to realize how good it was to be an ordinary person. And suddenly he felt a strong desire to be an Indian villager surrounded by meek cattle rather than a King with a frightened army.

The King's companion was a wise Indian. At one time they stopped at the top of a small hill, sat down and gazed into the distance. From here the view was of a wonderful landscape, and all around them was greenery. They were wrapped in thought and silent. His companion asked: "Mighty King, I know you are very wise and learned, but I do not understand why you need all this. And why did you come here at all, so far from your home?"

The King did not answer him right away. After a while he calmly replied: "To outlive myself… To make the name of Macedonia indelible…"

He said these words absent mindedly, as if someone else was talking about him, not he himself.

The young commander and his companion spent a second and a third day too roaming the Indian villages. He was amazed by the many customs, he watched the villagers and their way of life, their unusual animals and the cult they had built around them. He all but ceased to think of the problem that troubled him.

On the third day they sat down in a field to rest. Some twenty cows grazed calmly near them. Then several villages riding elephants appeared at the other end of the field, heading towards them. And in this idyllic peace a small dog suddenly charged forward, barking at one of the cows. The frightened cow then alarmed all the other cows, and all of them started running headlong, creating a great noise and din. Surprised, the King jumped to his feet to see what was going on. And he noticed that the frightened cows were heading straight for the elephants, bolting towards them… But then the elephants took fright at the headlong stampede of the cows, so they turned, shook off the villagers sitting on their necks and started to flee blindly from the cows.

The Macedonian King was clearly excited by the rapid sequence of events. Suddenly, like lightning, a life saving thought flashed through his mind. He turned around and started to run back to his soldiers. His

companion was bewildered by his reaction and the speed with which he moved.

When they came to their encampment the guards very nearly stabbed him through with their spears, thinking he was an enemy charging at them with incredible speed. He was shouting breathlessly: "I know how we shall win! I know how we shall win!"

He went into his tent and started jumping around with joy like a child. The generals immediately gathered around him to see what had inspired such childlike joy in their commander.

Baffled, they got hold of the breathless interpreter, the Indian, who was running after the King. Took him by the throat and demanded to be told whether he had given some strange food to their King. Or perhaps he had taken some strange drink, to behave like this? But the King calmed down a little and ordered the army to be summoned before him. The generals came and all the soldiers to hear what their commander had to tell them, and he said: "Take all the gold we have won as spoil, and buy cows from the villagers in the surrounding countryside! Buy as many as possible… The more the better…"

This order shocked the generals and soldiers even more!

But seeing that their King was serious, they laid down their arms, put on Indian clothing and left to buy cattle from the villagers. The cows they bought were gathered in a vast meadow. Over the next ten days they collected a vast number of cows and bulls.

Then the King ordered the army to prepare for the fiercest of battles that was to take place soon. It would be the greatest battle, one human-kind would never again witness nor be able to forget.

And indeed it was…

But the soldiers were still confused… Yet remembering the experience of previous battles and seeing that special glitter the King had in his eyes before all major battles, nobody said or asked anything. They could sense it, their experience told them that behind all this there stood some great design of their King. The day and the place of the battle were already agreed. Compared to the enemy's army, the Macedonian army looked ridiculously small.

The King explained to the generals what he intended to do. And this only increased their scepticism and made them think that having finally realized how difficult and great was the battle awaiting them, he had simply taken leave of his senses. But they had to obey orders. And so the army drove the huge herd ahead of them, keeping their distance in the rear.

When they arrived at the battlefield, they saw in the distance the lances and elephants in the enemy's front line. Lined up in close ranks and ready to charge, they were a frightening sight.

Then the King ordered the soldiers to prod the cows and chase them about. The cattle, frightened by the goading of the spears, stampeded headlong towards the elephants. The herd was so big that the entire field was immediately wrapped in a cloud of dust that rose to the sky. The horrendous, unstoppable stampede hurtled towards the elephants. Unlike other battles, this time it was not the infantry in the first line of battle, but the cavalry, driving the cattle into that furious and inescapable stampede. As the panic stricken animals drew thundering nearer, the elephants turned back in alarm and began to run in panic, trampling and killing the enemy army. There was fearful panic in the enemy ranks, and the maddened cattle, together with the elephants, literally ground the infantry underfoot.

When the elephants had smashed the enemy army, the Macedonian cavalry charged the surviving infantry and cavalry and took them prisoner. All this happened so quickly that the Macedonian phalanx did not have time to grasp how they had won when they had not even moved from their position!

In this battle, for the first time the Macedonian King was not at the head of his troops, but supervising the attack from the rear. Once the noise of the deadly, unstoppable stampede of the animals had abated and the clouds of dust settled down, the Macedonian pipes and drums were heard playing, heralding the festivities to mark their victory in the greatest battle in the history of humankind, one in which not one Macedonian soldier was killed.

They say that even two thousand five hundred years later the story of this battle is still recounted in India.

## LOVE CONQUERS ALL

At one time, centuries ago, Macedonia was a very powerful state. It had become such thanks to its strong and wise King, who had united the regions in his territory that had been at odds. He promoted the economy and culture. He made his people rich. And he gave them the vision that only thus could they conquer the whole world.

When he met his death, his youngest son was proclaimed his successor to the throne. Even as a child, he had listened to what his father told him and was thrilled by his ventures. He was also imbued with his father's idea that all should live in a single state in which each of the different peoples would develop freely. When he himself became King, he continued in his father's foot steps. And he set out to conquer the world.

The young King had also learned from his father that no enemy was invincible. No matter how mighty, each had its weakness. Sometimes what appeared at first sight to be the enemy's greatest strength could, if the proper tactics were used, be turned into their greatest weakness. All one had to do was discover it, in order to win a victory. He had also learned that others will follow you only if you yourself set an example by your own behaviour and courage. That only sincerity and care for each individual soldier keeps an army loyal. But also that only through great respect towards an enemy can a victory be won.

Inspired by his father's ideas, the young Macedonian King was fearless. For him, there was no invincible enemy. He was so successful in his battles that he truly made his generals euphoric. The army adored him and he managed to win great victories with minimal casualties. Even in situations which others considered hopeless, impossible and desperate, he was able to find the way to victory.

Soon his people began to see him as the son of a god, or as a god himself. He was young and enthralled by the great idea. But he was also very down-to-earth and accessible to all his people, for his father's words and thoughts always resounded in his mind.

The young King's great victories and conquests of new territories and peoples happened in rapid succession. The Macedonians advanced towards the East, in the belief that somewhere there was the end of the

world. The King was convinced that they would reach that end, and then they would have conquered the whole world.

On that journey the Macedonian army also entered the territory of today's Afghanistan. In addition to the rough terrain, the high mountains, the impassable gorges and rivers, the Macedonians encountered a very strong enemy, unlike any other they had encountered before. They fought in small groups, from ambush, with quick attacks and even quicker retreats. They were exceptionally skilful and brave warriors. Fearless. The Macedonians were used to fighting with great, strong armies where it took them one or two battles to triumph victoriously, subject that people and territory and move on.

This time it was different. They stopped here. They were stuck. The Macedonian army was under constant attack from this side or that. By the time they had positioned their formations, the enemy would have disappeared, only to reappear a few moments later in a new attack from a different direction. And so it went on and on. Day and night. The number of Macedonian casualties was rising, and the enemy was virtually inaccessible.

Great tension, insecurity and anxiety grew in the ranks of the army. The Macedonians had no stratagem to use against this kind of military tactics. They felt confused and impotent.

This was a completely new situation for the young but clever King. He too was taken aback by this style of combat which he had never experienced. He refused to admit it even to himself, but the truth was that he felt powerless. The enemy's tactics were so efficient that the growing feeling of powerlessness was driving him insane. He began to doubt even the idea of conquering the entire world, because he felt that this people was unconquerable. He also began to doubt his father's words that every adversary has a weakness and it is simply a matter of finding it.

With these uneasy feelings in his heart, he wanted to know more and more about the kind of man his opponent was, about this king who managed to evolve such efficient military tactics and about how he managed to train such valiant and skilful warriors. The more he learned about the wisdom of the king, the greater the respect he felt for him. He was so fascinated by the information he gathered about this man, that he simply discarded any idea that even the strongest enemy could be defeated as impossible. For the first time in his life, the invincible Macedonian King felt defeated.

The young King's demeanour changed as well. While his generals were overwrought and unnerved, holding gatherings, discussing and arguing among themselves about what to do and how to fight this army, the King was unnaturally calm. They found this strange, because he appeared to have no interest in finding a way out of the difficult situation they had got into. All he did was summon the Afghans to tell him about the various undertakings of their king. He was bewildered. He felt exactly as he had when he was a child and the Macedonians were telling him about the ventures of his famous father. That which he had feared most – to be defeated – now no longer seemed so terrible. He actually felt well. So, he would be defeated by a military leader who was wiser than him, and than his father. Indeed, he became convinced that even his father would not have been able to find an answer to the adversary's tactics…

In this melancholy mood he even started thinking of how he wished for a son who would be better and wiser than him, who would have all the qualities he was told the rival king possessed. He was completely lost.

The enemy's attacks did not cease. Macedonian soldiers were killed every single day. The increasing uncertainty that was spreading through the ranks further worsened the situation. The generals were already whispering among themselves that something was definitely wrong with their King, that he had lost touch with reality and nothing mattered to

him any more. Not even how many of his soldiers were killed, or how badly injured they were …

Meanwhile, the Macedonian King sat in his tent surrounded by Afghans who were recounting the achievements of their king. And one day, while telling him how wise and strong the great Afghan king was, an old man touched on the subject of the weakness of this king… The absorbed Macedonian King heard the translation of the word 'weakness' and instantly his eyes opened. The old man went on to tell him that the king had only one daughter who received special care and was always kept as far as possible from places where wars were waged…

At that moment the Macedonian King stopped listening and leapt from his seat like a horse suddenly spurred to a gallop. He rushed to his headquarters, where he found his generals sunk in despair. Seeing their King they jumped to their feet, surprised and perplexed. It was a long time since they had last seen him like this, with shining eyes and full of an energy so strong that where he walked it felt as if a wind was blowing.

"We shall win! I know how we shall win!" the King shouted at the top of his voice. The generals looked at him and listened as he explained his strategy, but could not grasp the idea… How were they going to win by what he suggested? And yet they could recognize his father in his glittering eyes and gesticulations. That was exactly how he had acted when he had a plan which was, to them, totally incomprehensible and impossible. But in the end it was always a plan that led to victory. Therefore, their skin bristling, they listened and nodded their heads, and even though they were not completely convinced, they nevertheless rejoiced to see him so spirited again.

The King ordered his most devoted generals and a hundred chosen soldiers to change into ordinary clothes of the kind worn by the natives. And also to take with them the most beautiful and valuable gold and jewels they had seized as booty in previous conquests.

Thus equipped, they set out for the other end of the country, led by the young King, to find the daughter of the Afghan king. They were to take her captive and thus force the invincible adversary to surrender under the threat that should he not do so they would kill the princess.

After many days riding at the gallop, during which they passed through many dangerous and nearly impassable places, they reached the other end of the kingdom. No one here suspected them of being enemies, and many did not even know there was a war going on.

The newcomers were welcomed warmly and with some curiosity, for they looked different, with their strange fair skin and different coloured hair.

The Macedonian King, his generals and the soldiers introduced themselves as merchants trading in expensive and valuable goods, and as such quickly learned the whereabouts of the princess's palace.

When they reached the palace, they saw it was secured by numerous guards who were armed to the teeth. The Macedonian King's generals turned to him. What now? He laughed and said: "You're merchants, aren't you, not generals... So do as merchants would do..."

The next day they went to the palace gates but were stopped by the guards. Then they opened their chests and took out the most beautiful gold jewellery set with all possible precious stones. The young princess happened to see this from the window of her chamber and ordered that the merchants be allowed to enter the palace. The officer in charge of her security did not want to allow this, but the princess's curiosity was so great that he had to obey.

The disguised Macedonian King and his party, together with their bursting chests, were taken before the princess. As he clumsily tried to play the part of a merchant opening his stock of jewellery, the King straightened up to display something he was holding in his hand and suddenly seemed to have lost his tongue… In front of him stood the princess, a girl with a wonderful figure, long black hair and large transparent green eyes, the colour of the water in the river he loved to bathe in when he was in Macedonia…

Our King became so flustered he seemed not to know where he was or what he was doing, but continued clumsily taking objects and jewellery from the chest to show her, and kept dropping them… He was so confused that everyone in the room started to laugh aloud. But the princess caught the jewellery falling from his hands, not looking at the objects but staring at him as if he were a vision…

Later the Macedonian generals reported that everything happened like in a fairy tale where two young people set eyes on each other once and never part again. As if both of them had been dreaming of this meeting, constantly searching for the other, but never imagining that they would meet here, at the end of the world. They immediately burned with love for each other.

While happy to see their King had finally fallen in love, his generals were worried that this development would thwart their plan …. The plan the King himself had devised and explained to them, according to which the princess was to be killed if the enemy king did not surrender.

The couple spent the following weeks together, and then the King announced that he was going to marry the princess and ordered that all those of importance in the country should be invited to the royal wedding. And he also ordered that the princess's father, his greatest enemy, should be invited. And be welcomed with the highest military honours, such as those with which the Macedonians would welcome his father on his return from some victorious campaign. And the King and the princess and all his companions set out together to join the Macedonian army at the other end of the country.

The news that his beloved daughter was in the hands of the Macedonians was a heavy blow to the King of Afghanistan. He knew that unless he went and gave himself up she would be killed. So he ordered all attacks to cease, and at the head of his army, shields lowered and spears drag-ging on the ground, he led them to the city where the Macedoni-

ans had established themselves. He had only one thought in his mind, the hope that when he surrendered they would spare his daughter…

But the sight that met them when they arrived at the city left them speechless. The entire Ma-cedonian army was lined up in parade uni-form to greet the enemy with highest military honours. The king could not hide his delight when he saw his beloved daughter standing in the loving embrace of the young Macedonian King. Tears trickled down his face as he opened his arms to hug his son-in-law. And the Macedonian King felt as if it was his beloved father who held him in his arms.

The reception then turned into a great celebration by the Macedonian army. And it was in-deed a unique celebration in which conquerors and conquered celebrated together. Love had conquered all.

About the author:

Zan Mitrev was born in Štip, where he completed his primary and secondary education. He graduated from the Faculty of Medicine in Skopje, and specialized in surgery in Zagreb and cardiovascular surgery in Germany. He worked as a cardiac surgeon in Frankfurt and Zurich, and in 2000 opened the first private hospital in Macedonia. In 1997, in Frankfurt, he was the first Macedonian to carry out a heart transplant. Now, in the words of the author, he has performed surgery on the spiritual heart of Macedonia...

This is the context of this book as well, with 8 stories about two great Macedonian figures, as his contribution to future generations.

Zan Mitrev

MACEDONIAN STORIES ABOUT PHILIP AND ALEXANDER

Book 1

Translated from the Macedonian by:
Ljubica Arovska

Translation edited by:
Peggy Reid

Illustrator
Igor Jovcevski

Computer graphics
Slobodan Kostovski
Daniel Veljanovski

2012